Contents

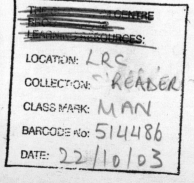

Introduction

'I can't leave prison when the government is killing black people. I don't want to use violence, but President Botha has to stop it. He has to stop apartheid. He has to talk to the ANC.'

Nelson Rolihlahla Mandela's life is the story of a country boy and his fight for the black people of South Africa. He was born in 1918 in the village of Mvezo in the Transkei. He was the youngest son of the chief of the Xhosa tribe in Mvezo. But when Nelson was a baby, the government took away his father's land, animals and job. So Hendry Mandela took his four wives, four sons and nine daughters to Qunu. Hendry never went to school, but he sent his youngest son to an English church school. There, the teacher gave him an English name: Nelson. But when the boy was nine years old, his father died. His mother took him to the home of Chief Jongintaba. This was the first of many changes in his life.

The chief sent his son, Justice, and Nelson to very good English church schools, and Nelson was a good student. But when he was twenty-two years old, he had problems with the chief and with the university. Nelson and Justice ran away to Johannesburg. There, Nelson learned about life for blacks, about apartheid and the ANC.

The government wanted to stop the work of the ANC and Mandela, so they put him in prison for twenty-seven years. But he did not stop protesting. When he left prison, he did not stop fighting apartheid. Presidents and leaders from round the world wanted to help Mandela. On 27 April 1994, the people of South Africa had a black leader, President Nelson Mandela. This is the story of one man – a freedom fighter and one of the world's most important leaders.

Nelson Mandela

COLEEN DEGNAN-VENESS

Level 2

Series Editors: Andy Hopkins and Jocelyn Potter

Pearson Education Limited
Edinburgh Gate, Harlow,
Essex CM20 2JE, England
and Associated Companies throughout the world.

ISBN 0 582 461650

First published 2001

Second impression 2001

Copyright © Coleen Degnan-Veness 2001
Map of South Africa by Janos Marffy

Typeset by Pantek Arts Ltd, Maidstone, Kent
Set in 11/14pt Bembo
Printed in Spain by Mateu Cromo, S.A. Pinto (Madrid)

Published by Pearson Education Limited in association with
Penguin Books Ltd, both companies being subsidiaries of Pearson Plc

Acknowledgements:
All photographs reproduced courtesy of Link Picture Library.

For a complete list of the titles available in the Penguin Readers series please write to your local
Pearson Education office or to: Marketing Department, Penguin Longman Publishing,
5 Bentinck Street, London, W1M 5RN.

South Africa 1652–1994

In 1652, white Dutch people (Boers) went to the Cape in South Africa, and they took land from the Africans. They took the men from the African tribes because they wanted workers. In 1795, the British arrived. From 1803–1815 there was fighting in Europe. When it ended, the British got the Cape. There were problems between the British and the Boers (or 'Afrikaners'), and from 1899–1902 they fought. The British won, but in 1910 they wanted to work with the Afrikaners. So the Cape, Natal, the Orange Free State and the Transvaal had one government with an Afrikaner president.

At this time in South Africa, there were 4,020,000 Africans, 1,280,000 whites, 150,000 Indians and 530,000 coloureds (half white). White people made the laws. One law was the Pass Law. Africans had to carry a pass book and could not go from one town to another town without it. They had to show it to policemen when they asked for it. Years later, when blacks did not carry their pass books, the police arrested them.

Africans had to live in places for 'Blacks Only', but they worked for white people. Whites had good jobs and blacks had bad jobs. They lived by different laws. The only schools for black children were church schools. Other children went to government schools.

From 1948, 'apartheid' was the word for these laws and this way of life. The ANC* fought apartheid and they won this fight in 1994.

*ANC (African National Congress): a political organization of black people; it started in 1912.

Map of South Africa

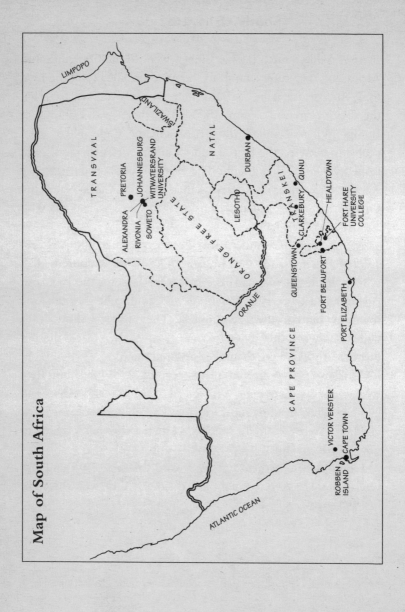

Chapter 1   From Country Boy to City Lawyer

1918	18 July Nelson Mandela is born in Mvezo.
1934	He goes to school at Clarkebury.
1937	He goes to school at Healdtown.
1939	He goes to university at Fort Hare.
1941	He runs away to Johannesburg.
1942	He leaves university.
1943	His first protest is in Alexandra.
1943	He goes to university at Witwatersrand.

A happy boy. When he was a child, Nelson Mandela was very happy. He lived with his mother and sisters in Qunu, and his father lived with them for one week every month. His father's three other wives and their children were also his family. Nelson enjoyed the freedom of life in the country. But when his father died, his mother took him to the home of Chief Jongintaba in the town of Mqhekezweni. It was wonderful there. People had money and wore nice clothes. And the chief's son, Justice, was a good 'brother' to him.

When Nelson was sixteen years old, the chief took him to school in Clarkebury. Justice studied and lived there too. Nelson had to study hard because the chief wanted him to work with the leaders of the Xhosa tribe. Nelson met people from other places, but he did not understand their ways. He was a country boy and his world was small.

There is one very important day in the life of a Xhosa boy. When they are sixteen years old, they stop being boys. Nelson sat on the ground with the other boys. He was afraid of the cut from the old man's knife. But when it came, he waited a very short time. Then he shouted the important words, 'I am a man!' Mandela remembers this day and says, 'I was not as strong as the other boys.'

Then Chief Meligqili spoke. He said to the young men and their fathers, 'Our sons sit there, flowers of the Xhosa tribe. But they are not men . . .' He spoke about the white men's laws for black men in South Africa. The men listened to him and were angry. Nobody wanted to hear these words. Nelson liked the white men because they built schools for his people. At that time, he did not understand the chief's words. Some years later, he understood very well.

Nelson's next school, Healdtown, was in Fort Beaufort. In the 1800s, the British took this place from the Xhosa people and killed many great Xhosa fighters. Two of them died in the prison at Robben Island near Cape Town. Later, Robben Island was very important in Nelson's life, too.

Important changes. At Healdtown, Nelson met a teacher from the Sotho tribe, and his wife was a Xhosa. At that time in South Africa, Africans did not marry people from different tribes. But Nelson's ideas started changing after he met that teacher. And for the first time, he started being an African, not only a Xhosa.

When he was twenty-one years old, he went to university at Fort Hare. Some of Africa's greatest thinkers studied there. Nelson studied law, politics and English. But at the end of his third year, a lot of the students protested because they wanted better food. They wanted the new leaders of their student organization to make changes. They wanted Nelson to be one of their leaders. The authorities did not like their protest. But Nelson understood the students and tried to help. The president of the university told him, 'Go home for the holidays and change your ideas.' Nelson did not want to change, but he wanted to finish his studies. He had one more year. What could he do?

Nelson started being an African, not only a Xhosa.

He and Justice went home for the holidays and Nelson talked to Chief Jongintaba about this problem. The chief was very angry and said, 'You will change your ideas and go back to Fort Hare.' But some weeks later, he talked to the young men again about their future. They were not ready for his words.

'I am near the end of my life,' he told them. 'I have to make plans for my sons, so you are going to marry – now.'

They did not want to marry! Nelson and Justice ran away from home and went to Johannesburg. The chief was very angry. It was a dangerous journey for young black men without a pass or a letter from their parents. The police could arrest them. After some difficult months, Nelson got a job with some lawyers in Johannesburg, and he studied at night. He did not have much money at this time.

At the end 1941, the chief visited Nelson in Johannesburg, but he did not talk about the past, only about the future. It was a happy meeting. Then, in 1942, Chief Jongintaba died.

At the end of 1942, Nelson finished his university studies. He was very happy because not many black people went to university.

The ANC. Mandela learned about the ANC from his new friends Walter Sisulu and Gaur Radebe. He went to some ANC meetings. Then, in August 1943, Radebe and Mandela, with 10,000 other people, protested because the Alexandra bus company wanted people to pay more money for bus tickets. They did not use the bus company for nine days. There was no violence, and the bus company did not get more money. Mandela started thinking about protests for more changes for black Africans.

He studied law at Witwatersrand University from 1943–9. It was the best English-language university in South Africa, and Mandela was the only black student in the law school. But he had to work at the same time, and in the end he left Witwatersrand. He did not finish his studies.

Chapter 2   The Freedom Fighter

1944	Mandela marries Evelyn Mase.
1946	His first son, Thembi, is born.
1947	His first daughter is born, but dies nine months later.
1952	His second son, Makgatho, is born.
1952	He starts a new law office with Oliver Tambo.
1952	June 26 is the Day of Protest.
1953	His second daughter, Makaziwe, is born.
1956	On December 6, the police arrest Mandela; Evelyn leaves.

Husband and lawyer. Mandela married Evelyn Mase some months after they met at the home of his friend, Walter Sisulu. She was a good wife and mother to their children, but she was not interested in politics. Later, this was a problem between them. Mandela was a student when they married. But he was on the way to a very different life.

He worked very hard in a law office and for the ANC. One day his five-year-old son, Thembi, asked his mother, 'Where does Dad live?' Mandela came home late at night and left early every morning. He wanted to see his family. But one man could not organize protests for the country and be at home with his family.

Then, in 1950, the government made more apartheid laws. They took land from the blacks, the coloureds and the Indians. More than 50,000 black people lived in Sophiatown in Johannesburg. It was an important town for the blacks, but the whites took it. The next year, the government made more apartheid laws.

In 1951, Walter Sisulu wanted the ANC to work with the coloureds and the Indians in their protest. He spoke to Mandela,

Mandela married Evelyn Mase.

but Mandela did not like this idea. The other ANC leaders liked it, so Mandela changed his ideas. The ANC organized a protest. They told the government, 'Change six apartheid laws or we'll protest again.' The government did not listen.

Mandela organized protesters. 'This will be dangerous,' he told them, 'but you can't use violence. Perhaps the police will use violence, but you can't.' Mandela went to Durban and spoke to 10,000 people. He told them, 'The world will see us and listen.'

The Day of Protest. The Day of Protest was the ANC's first protest across the country. 'Use white people's toilets, trains, waiting rooms and post offices,' they told blacks. The government was angry and the police arrested Mandela, his Indian friend, Yusuf Cachalia, and many other protesters. They were in prison for two days. Eight thousand people went to prison in the next five months. There was no violence and Mandela was happy with the protests.

In 1952, Mandela started a new law office in the centre of Johannesburg with his friend, Oliver Tambo. It was the only office of black lawyers in South Africa. Every day, they listened to the thousands of problems of black people.

The government wanted to stop Mandela and the ANC, so sometimes the government banned Mandela and other important ANC people from meetings. Sometimes they could not leave Johannesburg for nine months, or for two years, or for five years, for meetings with other ANC people.

The president of the ANC at that time was Chief Luthuli, a Zulu. In 1954, Nelson Mandela, Walter Sisulu, Chief Luthuli and other important ANC people started a new organization for blacks, Indians and coloured people. This new organization, the 'Congress of the People', wanted everybody to have the same laws as white people.

Kliptown. In June 1955, there was a meeting of the Congress of the People in Kliptown, near Soweto, and 3,000 people went to it. Earlier, the government banned Mandela and Sisulu from meetings for two years. But the two men drove to Kliptown and watched. They had to be careful. Suddenly, the police came. They stopped the meeting, but there was no violence. Mandela and Sisulu drove back to Johannesburg and the police did not catch them.

In September 1955, Mandela's two-year ban ended. He went to the Transkei and visited family and friends for two weeks. But he also wanted to talk to ANC people in different places about plans for the organization. In 1956, the police tried to stop Mandela's meetings with the ANC across the country, but this time he did not listen to the authorities.

Arrests. On 5 December 1956, the police went to his house early in the morning and for forty-five minutes they looked everywhere for his papers. They arrested Mandela in front of his wife and children and took him away in a police car. Mandela sadly remembers his children's faces.

That day, the police arrested 144 people. A week later, they took Walter Sisulu and eleven other people to Johannesburg Prison. They were there for four days. People across the country protested; people across the world protested, too.

At the same time, there were problems in the Mandela family. Evelyn did not want a freedom fighter for a husband. She left him when he was in prison. She took the children with her.

Chapter 3   Treason Trial and a New Wife

1957	Mandela meets Winnie Nomzamo Madikizela.
1958	He marries Winnie. The Treason Trial begins.
1958	Their first daughter, Zenani, is born.
1960	The police kill sixty-nine protesters at Sharpeville.
1960	The ANC protest the Pass Laws.
1960	On 8 April, the government bans the ANC and the PAC.
1961	On March 29, the Treason Trial ends.

On trial for treason! On 19 December, the government thought of a new plan: put the prisoners on trial for treason. But the trial did not start for nine months, so the prisoners had to pay the government. Then they could go home – and wait.

Mandela met Winnie Nomzamo Madikizela in 1957 and married her a year later. She was sixteen years younger than him and very beautiful. She was not interested in politics, but her husband taught her. She went to meetings with him and met his friends. In a very short time, she was a political speaker and protester, too. She helped Mandela through these difficult months before the trial. She gave him hope and love.

The Treason Trial began in August 1958. The authorities moved it from Johannesburg to Pretoria because the ANC was weak there. Ninety-two men and women had a two-hour journey by bus to Pretoria every morning. The trial took them away from their jobs, so they lost money. But the trial brought black, Indian, coloured and white protesters into the same place – there were some white people in the ANC. They discussed ideas at lunch and they enjoyed the conversations. But the trial did not end for five years.

Winnie gave Mandela hope and love.

The PAC (Pan African Congress) started in April 1959. It wanted to help blacks too, but it did not want to work with Indians, coloureds and whites. It wanted blacks to leave the ANC and work with them. Mandela did not like the PAC's ideas. When the PAC organized a protest some days before an ANC protest, Mandela was angry.

Protest the Pass Laws! In Cape Town on 21 March 1960, 30,000 people protested with the PAC about the Pass Laws. The police used violence and killed two people. And in Sharpeville, the police killed sixty-nine blacks. They hurt 400 men, women and children. People in many countries round the world protested, because they were angry with the South African government.

Nelson Mandela, Walter Sisulu and two other ANC men discussed a new plan with Chief Luthuli. Chief Luthuli started a fire in the street in Pretoria. He put his pass book into the fire. Mandela did the same thing in front of hundreds of people and many newspaper photographers. Two days later, thousands of black people did the same as Chief Luthuli. There was violence in many places. Very quickly, the government made a new law: nobody could protest. They arrested Mandela and thirty-nine protesters.

They put these forty people in one small, dirty room in the prison. There was no toilet, no toilet paper, no beds, no food. Mandela protested. They got some very bad food and ate it with their hands. After thirty-six hours in the prison, Mandela left for the Treason Trial in Pretoria. Life was very strange. The prisoners could leave and go to their trial every day. Also, at weekends, Mandela could go to Johannesburg and work in his law office. A policeman took him there and brought him back to the prison. Winnie visited him in his office.

11

Ban the ANC! On 8 April 1960, the government banned the ANC and the PAC. Oliver Tambo quickly left the country and went to London. He worked for the ANC from there for thirty years.

Free them! After five long years, the Treason Trial ended. Mandela remembers the words, 'These men and women did not use violence and they did not want to change the government through the use of violence.' Mandela left prison, a free man.

Chapter 4   Time for Violence

1960	Mandela and Winnie's second daughter, Zindzi, is born.
1962	Mandela visits leaders of other countries.
1962	The authorities arrest him; he gets five years in prison.
1963	He goes to Robben Island.
1963	On 9 October, the Rivonia Trial begins.
1964	On 12 June, he gets life in prison.

A dangerous life. The ANC's work was very dangerous now, so Mandela had to start a new life. He wore his hair long and dressed in different clothes. He did not want the police to catch him. But he spoke to many people from the newspapers at this time. In the newspapers, they called him the Black Pimpernel.* He drove across the country and talked to many people about the ANC's work.

*Pimpernel: a name from a famous story about the Scarlet Pimpernel. The police could not catch this man.

'We'll have to use violence now,' Mandela and many of the ANC people thought. So Mandela started a new organization – the MK (Umkhonto we Sizwe). He did not want to kill people. He wanted to stop telephone calls and stop trains. He wanted to make the government weak.

The ANC wanted Mandela to go to an important meeting in Addis Ababa, Ethiopia, in February 1962. They had to have money for the MK. Winnie was afraid for her husband, but she understood. Mandela flew to Tanganyika (now in Tanzania). From there, he went to the meeting in Ethiopia, then to Egypt, Tunisia, Morocco, Mali, Guinea, Sierra Leone, Liberia, Ghana, Senegal and London. Some leaders gave him money, some did not.

Mandela was very happy when he saw London for the first time. He saw Oliver Tambo, and he met some important politicians there, too. Then he went back to Addis Ababa and learned more about fighting. But the ANC wanted him in South Africa, so he flew back home.

Freedom ends in Rivonia. On 5 August 1962, the police caught Nelson Mandela in a car outside Rivonia. People protested and shouted, 'Free Mandela!' His trial started on 22 October 1962, and Mandela wore his Xhosa tribal clothes. He wanted the world to see a black man under white men's law. On 7 November 1962, he got five years in prison. His friend Walter Sisulu got six years.

Boy or man? In prison, the authorities gave Mandela short trousers because black prisoners were only 'boys'. Mandela was angry and he protested. So the warders gave him long trousers – and a new room. For some weeks, Mandela saw no other prisoners. He had to stay in his room for twenty-four hours each day, with the light on. Every hour was a year to him. He had no

Mandela wore his Xhosa tribal clothes.

books, no paper, no pen – nothing. And after some weeks, Mandela said, 'I have to see people. I'll wear short trousers.'

In May 1963, they sent Mandela and three other political prisoners to Robben Island. There were about 1,000 prisoners and they were all black men. They had to work very hard.

On 11 July, the police found the MK's papers about plans for violence and they arrested other MK leaders. The authorities put Mandela and the other men on trial again in Pretoria. This time, it was worse than before. 'The government will kill us now, perhaps,' they thought.

The Rivonia Trial. The newspapers called this trial 'The Rivonia Trial' and it started on 9 October 1963. Mandela's wife and mother were at the trial and were afraid for him. The world heard about it on television and read about it in newspapers. In London, people protested. Many governments round the world wanted the South African government to free these men. The government lawyers said to the MK prisoners, 'You wanted to change the government, so you planned violence. You got money from other countries for guns. This is treason!'

On 12 June 1964, the trial ended with life in prison for Nelson Mandela, Walter Sisulu and five other ANC men. Mandela thought, 'We won't die,' and he smiled.

Chapter 5   Life in Prison

Robben Island. At Robben Island, the warders again gave short trousers to the black prisoners. Ahmed Kathrada, the only Indian and a good friend of Mandela, got long trousers. When Mandela protested, they gave him long trousers, too. But they did not give them to the other black prisoners, so Mandela gave them back. He was a leader in prison, and the men always wanted him to speak for them.

The prison rooms were small, wet and cold. The work was very hard and boring. A lot of the warders hated the prisoners, but Mandela could find good things in everybody – warders, too. But when the warders wanted the political prisoners to work harder, the men protested. They worked more slowly. It was a game. Sometimes the prisoners won; sometimes they lost.

The prisoners could write only one letter to their families every six months, and only 500 words in each letter. Sometimes family letters did not come. And when they came, some of the pages were not there. What could Mandela do? Protest!

Prison authorities want prisoners to feel weak, so the stronger men had to help the weaker men. Mandela was strong and he wanted to protest about the way of life in the prison. He always looked to the future.

Visitors. In the first months, there were some visitors. A photographer and a writer from the London *Daily Telegraph* newspaper arrived one day. Mandela spoke to the writer, then the photographer took a photo of Mandela and Walter Sisulu. Usually, they did not want anybody to take their photographs, but something about them in the English newspapers was perhaps a good idea. There were other visitors – lawyers from Britain and the United States. Were the prisoners from the Rivonia Trial well? Did they have food? The world was interested in them.

At the end of August, Winnie visited her husband. The room was small and there were five warders next to them. The Mandelas had to speak in English or Afrikaans and they could only speak about the family. Winnie had to leave after thirty minutes, and Mandela did not see her again for two years. He loved her very much, so this was very hard for him. Winnie had a lot of problems with the government, too. She was his wife and she also tried to change apartheid laws.

The photographer took a photo of Mandela and Walter Sisulu.

One day in the summer of 1965, the International Red Cross*
visited the political prisoners. Mandela told them, 'We want
better clothes for work and long trousers. We want better food,
bread for black prisoners and longer visits. We want to write
more letters to our families and we want to study. We have to
work very hard, and the prison authorities don't listen to us.' The
International Red Cross helped them. Later, Mandela told the
International Red Cross, 'We can't study without desks and
chairs.' They got them.

Prison life. Most of the prisoners from the Rivonia Trial wanted
to study. Mandela used books from the University of London.

*International Red Cross: an organization. It helps people in many countries.

But it was not easy because sometimes the books did not come for a long time. Sometimes, Mandela never saw the books. Some prisoners went to Mandela for help with the law. He had to be careful, but some men left prison early with his help.

Prisoners could not have newspapers, but the warders carried their sandwiches in newspaper. Sometimes, when they threw the newspapers away, the prisoners took them. But one day, a warder saw Mandela with a newspaper. For three days, he could not see or talk to anybody. And the warders did not give him food. The days without work and without other prisoners were the hardest thing about prison for Mandela.

Family. In his twenty-seven and a half years in prison, Mandela did not stop thinking about his family. In the spring of 1968 his mother visited, and later that year she died. Mandela was very sad because he could not see her one last time. In July 1969 his son, Thembi, died in a car accident. Again, he could not go home and be with his family. In 1978, his daughter Zeni married the son of the leader of Swaziland. Zeni and her husband brought their baby daughter to Mandela at Robben Island and he gave the baby the name Zaziwe – Hope.

Changes to prison life. In 1977 the authorities said, 'Political prisoners do not have to work,' so Mandela started a garden. He gave vegetables to the prison cook and to the warders. He enjoyed his garden very much. He also read a lot of books and played tennis. In 1980, the prisoners could have newspapers, and Nelson read, *Free Mandela!* It gave him hope.

Suddenly, in April 1982, the authorities moved Mandela, Walter Sisulu and two other men to Pollsmoor Prison in Tokai, Cape Town.

Chapter 6   Freedom

Pollsmoor Prison. Mandela and the other three men did not have their old friends with them now, and this was difficult. Their little room was wet, and Mandela protested. But in some ways, life was better at Pollsmoor. And it was easier for Winnie because she could visit her husband. Then, in May 1984, there was another change for prisoners. For the first time in twenty-one years, Mandela took Winnie in his arms.

On 31 January 1985, President Botha said for the sixth time, 'Mandela can have his freedom, but he and the ANC have to stop using violence.' Each time, Mandela said, 'The government uses violence with black people, 'so the ANC can't stop using violence. I can't leave prison when the government is killing black people. I don't want to use violence, but President Botha has to stop it. He has to stop apartheid. He has to talk to the ANC.' For the first time in twenty years, South Africans heard the words of Nelson Mandela, when his daughter Zindzi read them to the world on 10 February 1985.

Victor Verster. On 9 December 1988, they moved Mandela again. He went to Victor Verster, a prison fifty kilometres north-east of Cape Town. There, he had a very nice, large house.

In July 1989, Mandela's wife, children and grandchildren visited him. Then, on 5 July, Mandela got some new clothes for his first meeting with President Botha. Suddenly, a month later, Botha left the government and F. W. de Klerk was the new President. On 15 October 1989, President de Klerk freed Walter Sisulu and six other political prisoners. It was the beginning of the end of apartheid in South Africa.

On 2 February 1990, de Klerk stopped the ban on the ANC, the PAC and thirty-two other organizations. The political prisoners were free. Black leaders of political organizations began talks with the government.

The long walk to freedom. The government wanted to send Mandela to Johannesburg and free him there. But Mandela wanted to walk out of Victor Verster Prison, and he wanted the world to watch. He wanted to say 'Thank you' to his warders and 'Hello' to the people of Cape Town. On 11 February 1990, Mandela walked out of Victor Verster after more than 10,000 days in prison.

Chapter 7   President Mandela

1991	Mandela is President of the ANC.
1992	Mandela leaves Winnie.
1993	Mandela and de Klerk win the Nobel Peace Prize.
1994	Mandela is President of South Africa; apartheid ends.
1996	De Klerk leaves the government.
1998	Mandela marries Graça Machel.
1999	Mandela stops being President after his five years.

The politician. Mandela was seventy-one years old when he left prison. But he was not an old man. On 16 April, he happily listened and danced to music in London with 75,000 young people. Round the world, people watched Mandela dance to the music on their televisions. He told the people in London, 'We heard your songs about apartheid through the thick prison walls.'

Mandela visited many world leaders in Europe and North America because he wanted money and help for the ANC. In 1991, he was the new President of the ANC.

Problems with Buthelezi and de Klerk. In 1991, the Zulu and the Xhosa people fought, and thousands of people died. Mandela wanted Chief Buthelezi, the Zulu chief, to work with the ANC. The two leaders had to help their people. Mandela did not like de Klerk now, because de Klerk did not try to stop the fighting. Buthelezi did not listen to Mandela's ideas about de Klerk and his white government. Then, in July 1991, a writer for a South African newspaper got some important papers from the police. Mandela was right! The police helped the Zulu fighters because they wanted to stop the ANC. Important people in de Klerk's government lost their jobs.

When de Klerk, Buthelezi and Mandela were at a very important meeting in September 1991, Buthelezi did not take Mandela's or de Klerk's hand. He was not their friend.

Mandela's meetings with de Klerk were very difficult, but at the end of 1993, Mandela and de Klerk won the Nobel Peace Prize.* The two men were not friends, but that did not stop them. They worked for a new South Africa.

Mandela and de Klerk worked for a new South Africa.

*Nobel Peace Prize: Only the world's best leaders get this for their hard work.

Later, in May 1996, de Klerk made problems for Mandela's government again, because he did not want to work with the ANC. De Klerk left the government and he wanted Buthelezi to leave, too. But Mandela and Buthelezi worked better after de Klerk left.

Winnie and Graça. The two years after Mandela left prison were not happy times at home with Winnie. The newspapers wrote about their problems. Mandela loved Winnie, but she had another man. Mandela was very busy with the ANC, and again he did not have much time for his family. The ANC was his 'family', and some people in the ANC did not like Winnie now. She had problems with the law. Some people were violent, and a boy died. 'Was Winnie there when they killed him?' some people asked.

On 13 April 1992, Mandela left Winnie. On television, he sadly told the world, with his friends Walter Sisulu and Oliver Tambo next to him. This was a very bad time for him, and Winnie was unhappy, too. But later, Mandela met Graça Machel. Her husband, the President of Mozambique, was dead, and in 1998 she married Mandela on the day before his eightieth birthday. There were 2,000 people at the party, and Mandela was a happy husband again.

The new president. On 27 April 1994, a new South Africa was born. It was the end of apartheid. After a long, hard fight, many years in prison and a lot of talks with the white government, the new leader was a black man: President Nelson Mandela. His government was for everybody in South Africa, not only for the black people. He wanted everybody to work for a better country. He was not angry with the warders from prison, the white men or the old South African government. The whites were not afraid of him. He tried hard to work with de Klerk.

Mandela was a happy husband again.

Thabo Mbeki was the President of the ANC now. And when President Mandela finished his five years, Mbeki was the next President of South Africa. In Mandela's five years, there were many changes in South Africa for black people and white people. It was a difficult time, but the country grew. Many black people got better jobs and better homes. Other countries helped with money and jobs. There were more schools and better schools. Black people had cars.

But not everything was better. Many black people did not have a better life. Violence did not stop, of course, and in some ways it was worse. Many police left their jobs, and many white people left South Africa.

There are some problems in the new South Africa, but there is something more important there now – freedom, and hope. This is possible because one man loved his country and his people.

ACTIVITIES

South Africa 1652–1994 – Chapter 4

Before you read

1 Read about young Mandela in the box at the start of Chapter 1. Look at the names of places. Then find the places on the Map of South Africa.

2 Talk about the questions below in your language. Find the words in *italics* in your dictionary. They are all in the book.

  a How is the *chief* of a *tribe* different from a *president* of a country?

  b What is the job of a *warder* in a *prison*?

  c Do the police in your country *arrest* people when they *protest* in the streets?

  d Why is the *politics* in one country important to *governments* of other countries?

  e Are there *laws* about *treason* in every country, do you think? Why?

  f Do the *authorities ban* children from bars in your country?

  g Why do some people want to *organize violence*?

  h Why do hospitals and large companies sometimes give visitors a *pass*?

  i Who *leads* a *trial*?

  j What is more important: to have *land* or to be *free*?

  Now check these forms of some of the words above in your dictionary. Use them in sentences.

  freedom   lawyer   organization   political   politician   tribal   violent

After you read

3 What were the most important changes in Mandela's life in the years 1927–64? Why were they important?

4 Why did the government ban the ANC and the PAC?

5 Mandela and the MK used violence. Was this right or wrong, do you think? What did Mandela think?

Chapters 5–7

Before you read

6 Mandela was in prison for more than 10,000 days. Did he change his ideas about apartheid or violence, do you think?

After you read

7 What changes did Mandela fight for inside prison. Why?

8 Have a conversation with another student.

Student A: You are a visitor to South Africa. Ask Student B, 'How is your life different now?'

Student B: You are a black South African. Answer the visitor.

Writing

9 Look at the important dates in the boxes at the start of chapters 1–4. Write about Mandela's life from 18 July 1918–12 June 1964. Write about: Young Mandela, His Family Life, and His Political Life.

10 What did you know about South Africa before you read this book? What do you know now? Write about it.

11 When Mandela was in prison, his friend Oliver Tambo worked for the ANC in London. You are Mandela and you will be free tomorrow. Write a letter to Oliver. Tell him about your years in prison and your hopes for the future.

12 You work for a newspaper and you are going to South Africa. You will meet Nelson and Graça Mandela and ask them some questions. Write ten questions.

BESTSELLING
PENGUIN READERS

AT LEVEL 2

American Life

Audrey Hepburn

Black Beauty

The Call of the Wild

A Christmas Carol

The Last of the Mohicans

Mr Bean

The Railway Children

The Secret Garden

Treasure Island

Walkabout

White Fang